The Gate Contained

The Gate Contained

Poems by Christopher Guerin
Photographs by Michael Antman

Poems by Christopher Guerin   Photographs by Michael Antman

Paperback First Edition   ISBN 13: 979-8-218-27974-5

Voca Me Press   vocamepress@gmail.com

Designed & typeset by Sarah Koz. Set in Electra, designed by William Addison Dwiggins in 1935. Thanks to Nathan Matteson.

It's all perhaps a point of view,
Nothing is preternatural,
Just perpetually new,
A pride before there is no fall.

The Sonnets

The Essays

The Gate Contained is a joint effort, presenting sonnets and photographs by two artists side by side. Near the end, two essays by the artists attempt to put into context the unique nature of this volume, from their individual points of view. We invite the reader to jump to the essays if the first few pages raise more questions than answers. However, the book has been designed to be enjoyed, first page to last, with the hope that having viewed the sonnets/photographs, then the essays, the reader will want to go back through a second time.

The Sonnets

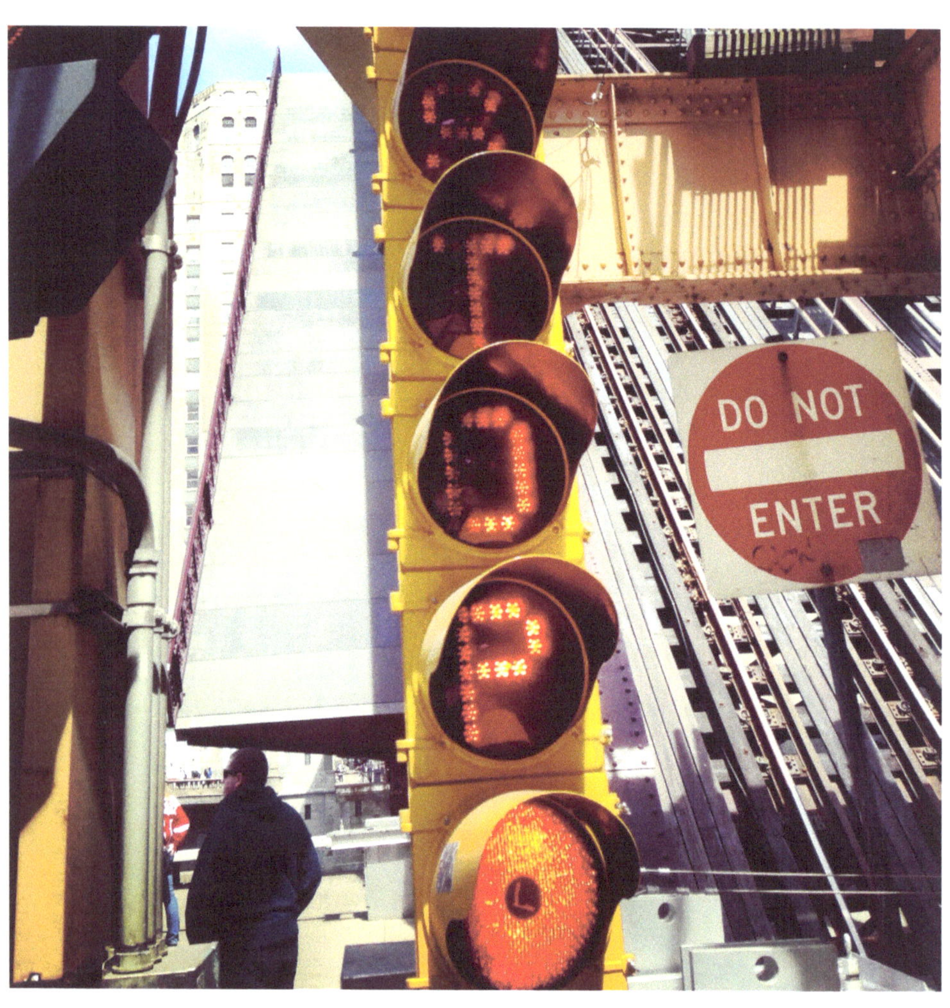
DO NOT
ENTER

The Crossing

The Chicago River drawbridge is up.
A moment of danger, repeated time
Overruled by STOP letters in their cups,
And a redundant Do Not Enter sign.
We wait because waiting is why we wait,
Nothing else in the world to do for long.
The fitful Spring air whistles through the grates
On the bridge, ageless sotto voce songs,
A sound of life beyond decay, so sweet.
The Windy City cannot hold its tongue.
The drawbridge collapses into a street,
And the crossings begin, of wheels and feet.
The boats below sail out toward Michigan,
Now crossing to then, again and again.

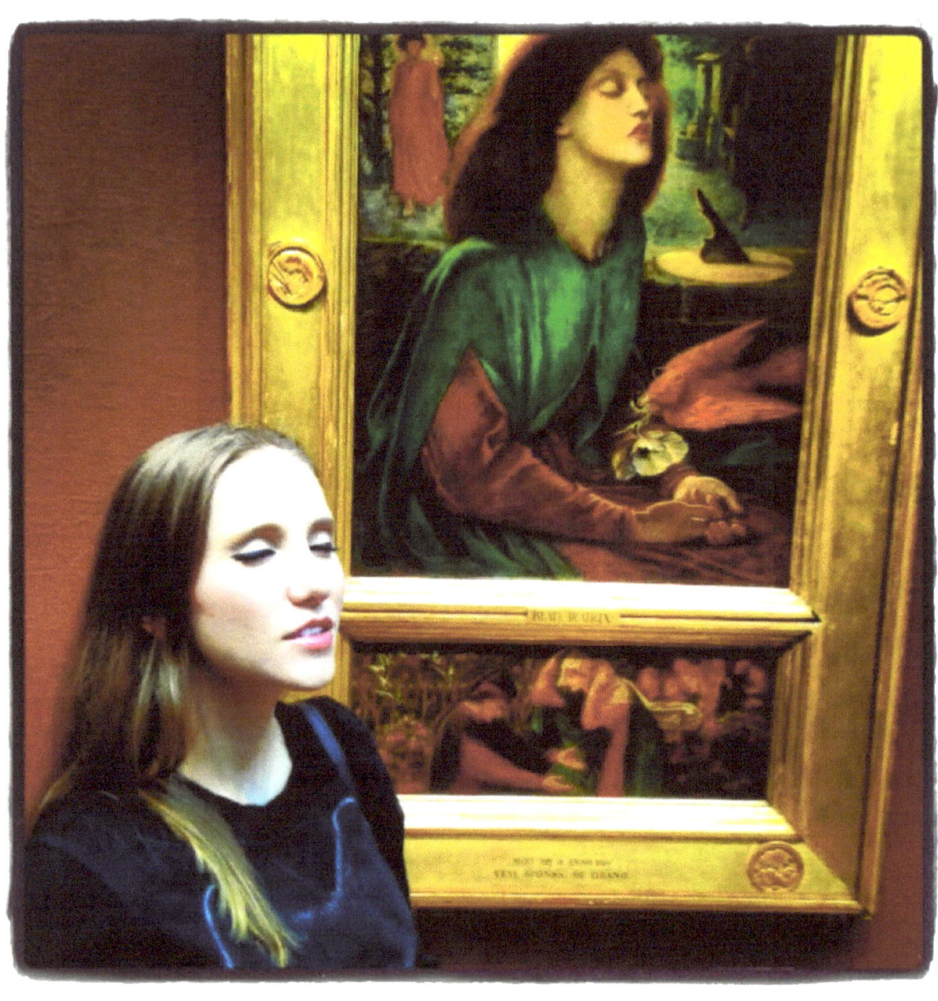

Irina Beatrix

Close your eyes and dream, dear Beatrix, dream.
The sundial at your wrist moves with the sun
And the stranger you meet each day, unseen
In the shadows, is yours, the only one:
He carries an ageless, cumbersome book,
In which he draws and draws your perfect face.
A face you've never recognized, he took
From you, idolizing the female race.
The scarlet dove drops a poppy into your lap—
You slip deeply into your alter consciousness.
A beautiful young woman closes her eyes too,
Centuries from now, and wakens you from your nap.
The death of your child is no longer meaningless.
Yes, you'll pass too—into a woman who is you.

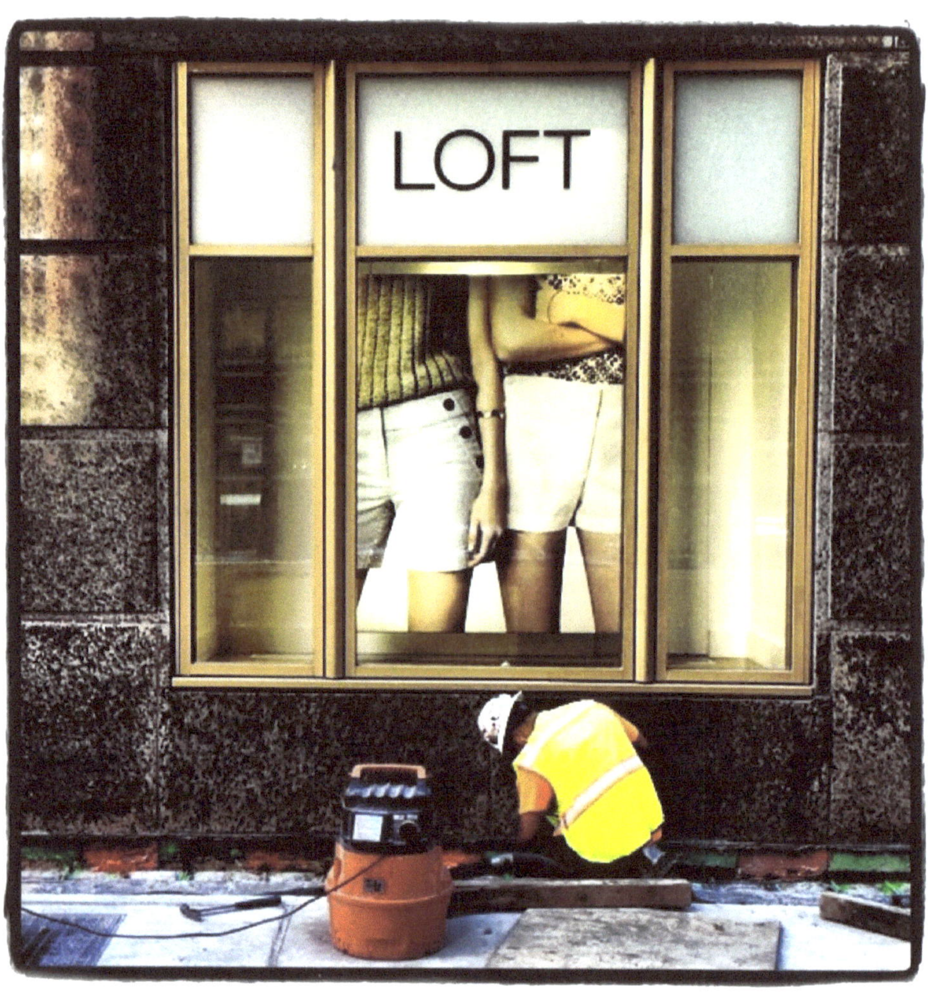
LOFT

Loft

The loft will fall if the foundations rot.
The window frames are already bending.
The masonry, pitted by ageless soot,
Awaits the inevitable rending
Of every pillar and joist underneath—
The spitting of mortar like broken teeth.
Two pairs of women's shorts are on display,
But the lonely workman ignores the show.
Naked legs would only be in his way.
He turns the electric vacuum to blow.
Now he must wait for everything to dry.
He looks up for the first time, starts to cry.
He's sundered by a sweet paralysis.
It's beautiful, he thinks, not sure what is.

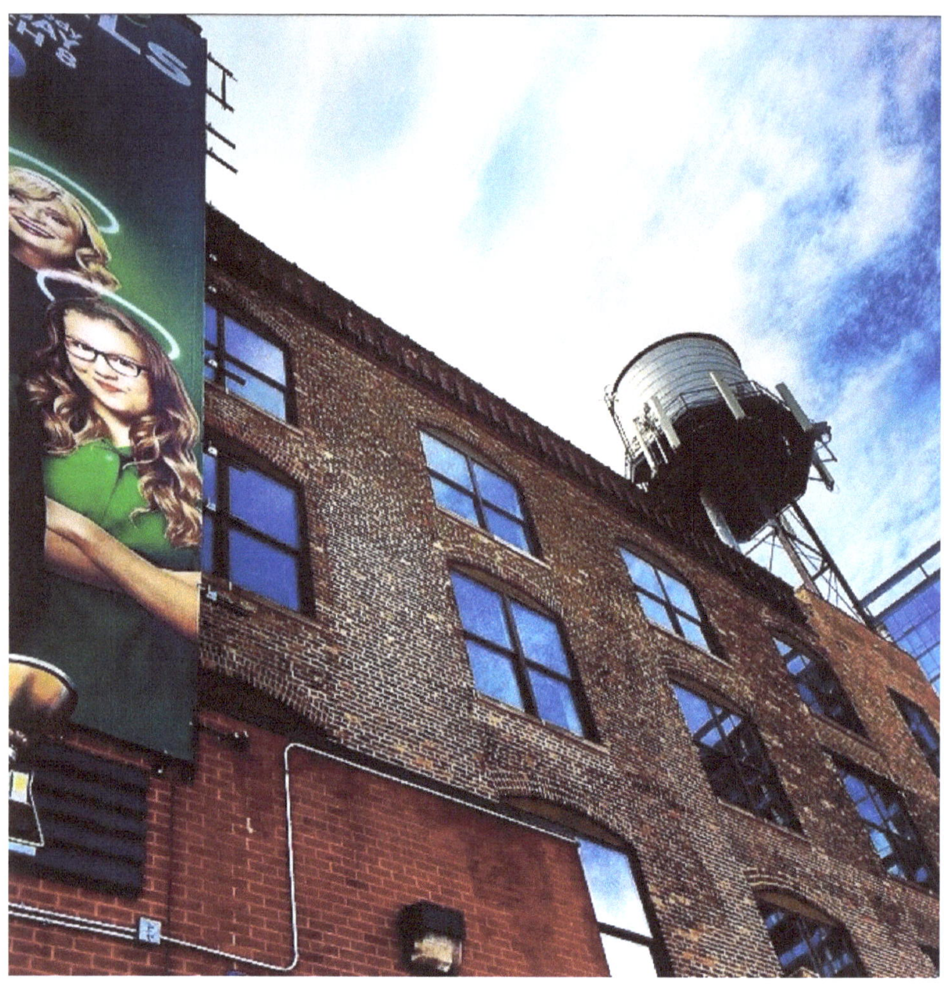

Dream Storage Tank

You feel layers of life of centuries
On Chicago streets, ubiquitous brick
Portraits and both mouthed and shouted stories
Of, not the dead, but spirits, pressed thick
Into the interstices of the air.
We know they are millions, huddling there,
So well hidden it's difficult to care.

How often tuck-pointed, the old brownstone,
Arched windows flattened by a glazier,
An old storage tank topped with a tin cone.
The lives within could not be hazier.
A haloed sweetheart with her mural grin,
Absolves spirit and flesh of painted sin.
The unseen millions breathe, breathe out, breathe in.

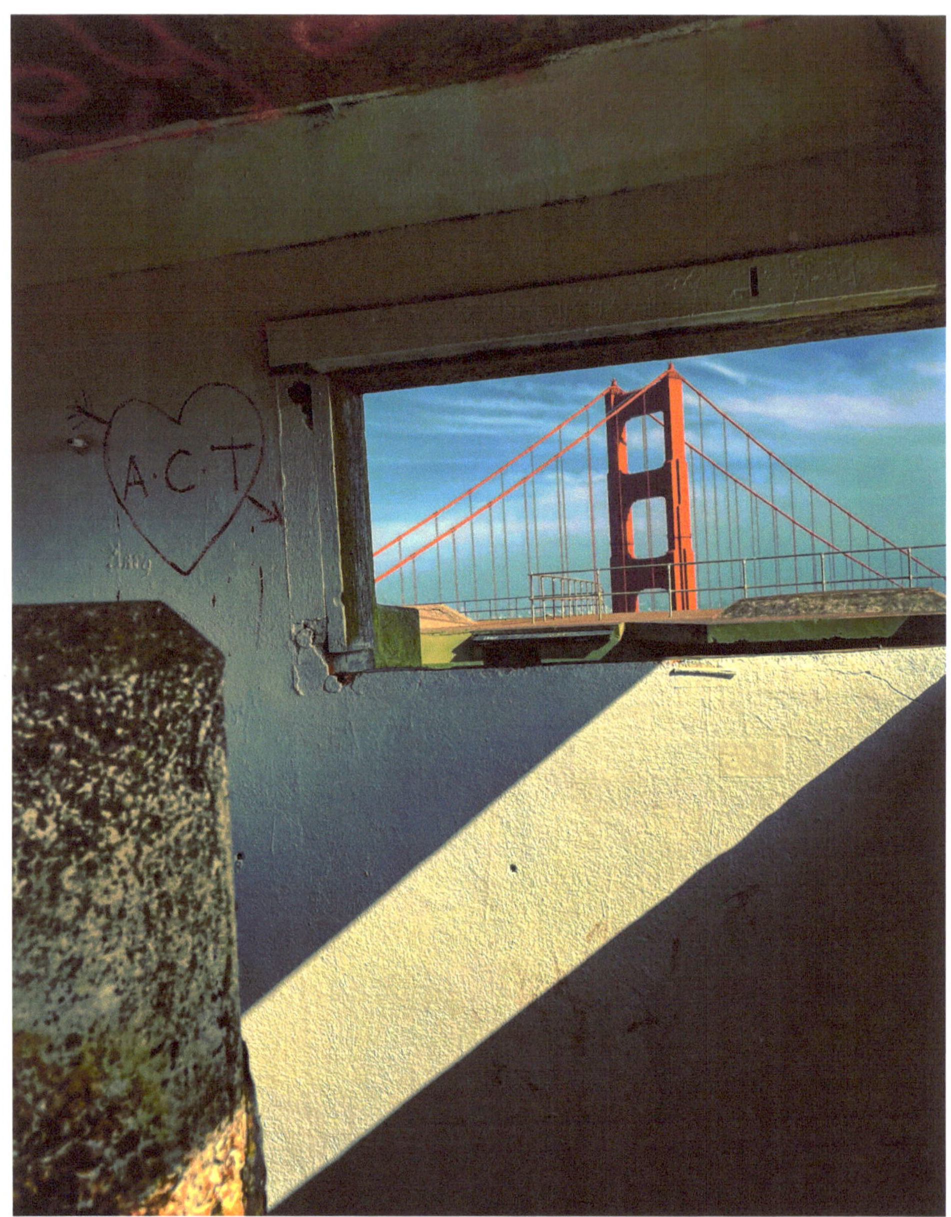
A·C·T

The Gate Contained

The visitor etched the word "act."
I don't know why inside a heart.
Call it a moment of found art,
All gesture and little impact.
We're staring out of a lost room
Through a cracked and discolored frame.
Bayside, metals and water boom.
The bright red bridge, in glorious bloom,
Guardian of what went and came,
Is like all things only a name.
With wrought iron and steel cable,
Men can create. They're capable
Of containing the setting sun
But must let go when day is done.

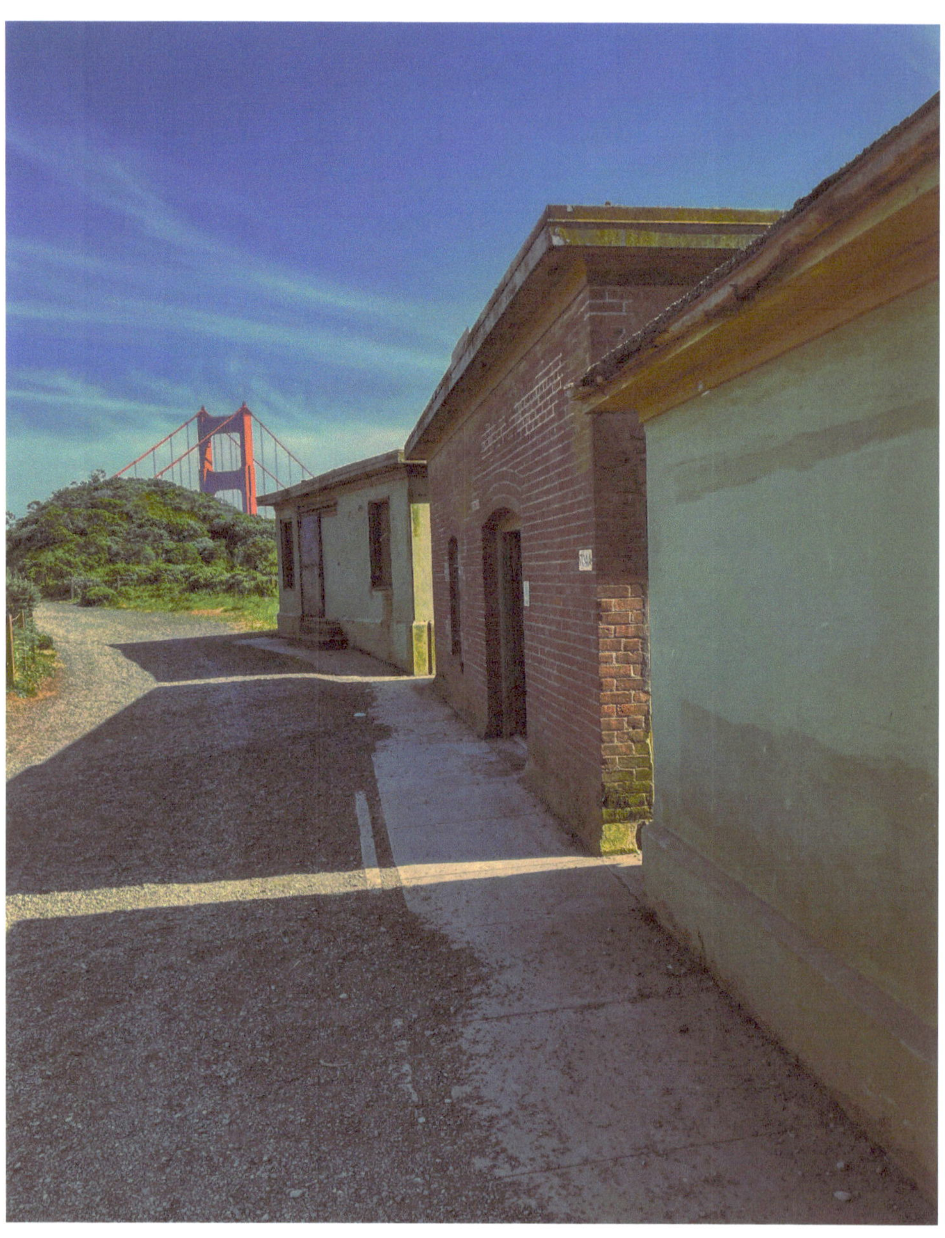

Sunfire in San Francisco

The slant light at sunset
Parses brick and shadow
As if they'd never met,
As if they didn't know
They are one and the same,
Congeries with one name.
That name is fire, and fire.
The bridge rises higher
To suspend fire and wire,
Reaching from sand to mire.
So old the paint and brick,
Cooling the shadow's wick.
All these make sun insane,
Absent mist, fog, or rain.

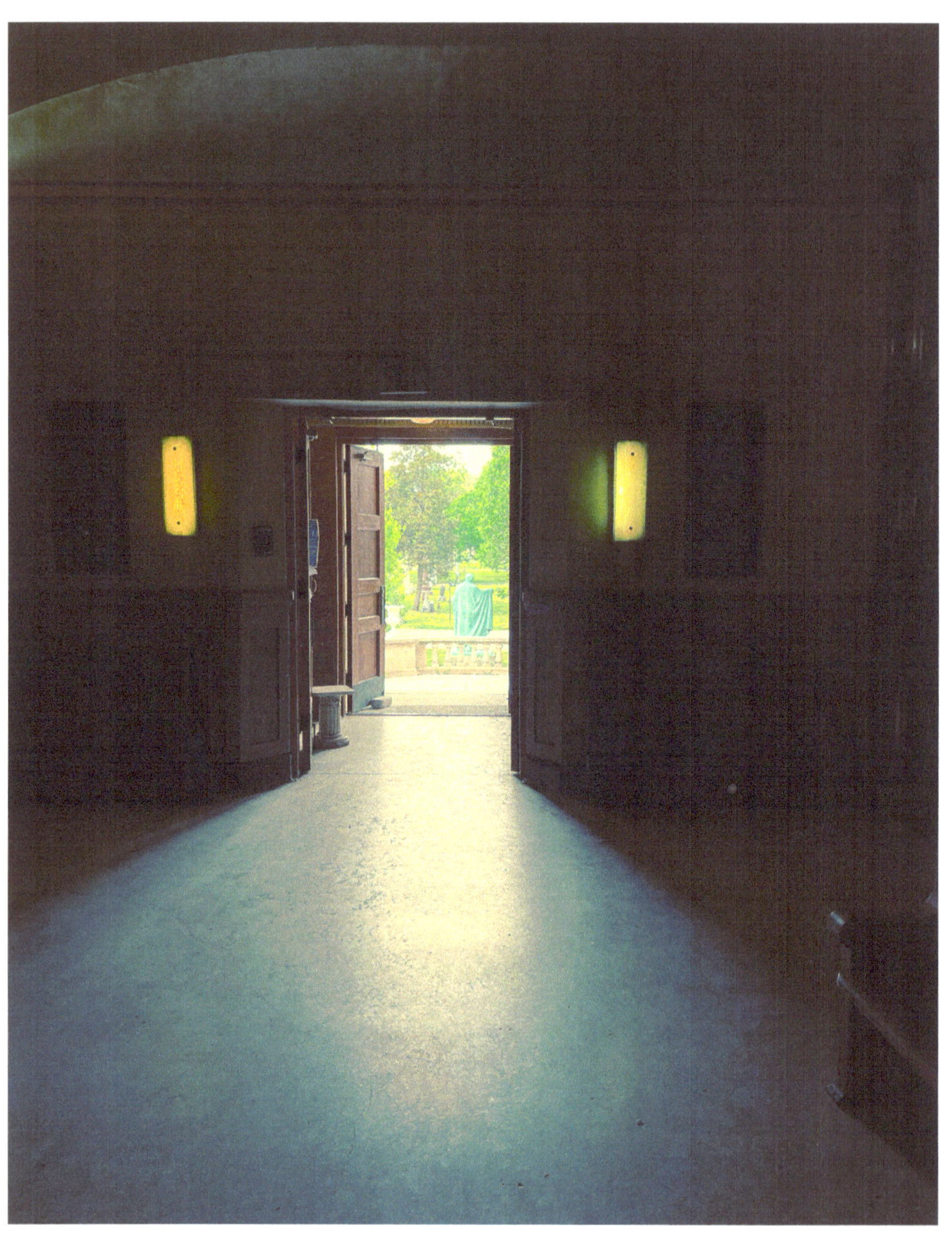

Entity

It's too soon to write about it.
I prefer Spinoza's spirit,
Its embodiment of rainbows,
No holier than house sparrows.
It's all perhaps a point of view,
Nothing is preternatural,
Just perpetually new,
A pride before there is no fall.
I stand inside an open door.
Indirect sunlight suffuses
The hallway with its sweet odor—
Even motes of dust have uses.
Outside a statue of mother
Asks, "Are you you, or some other?"

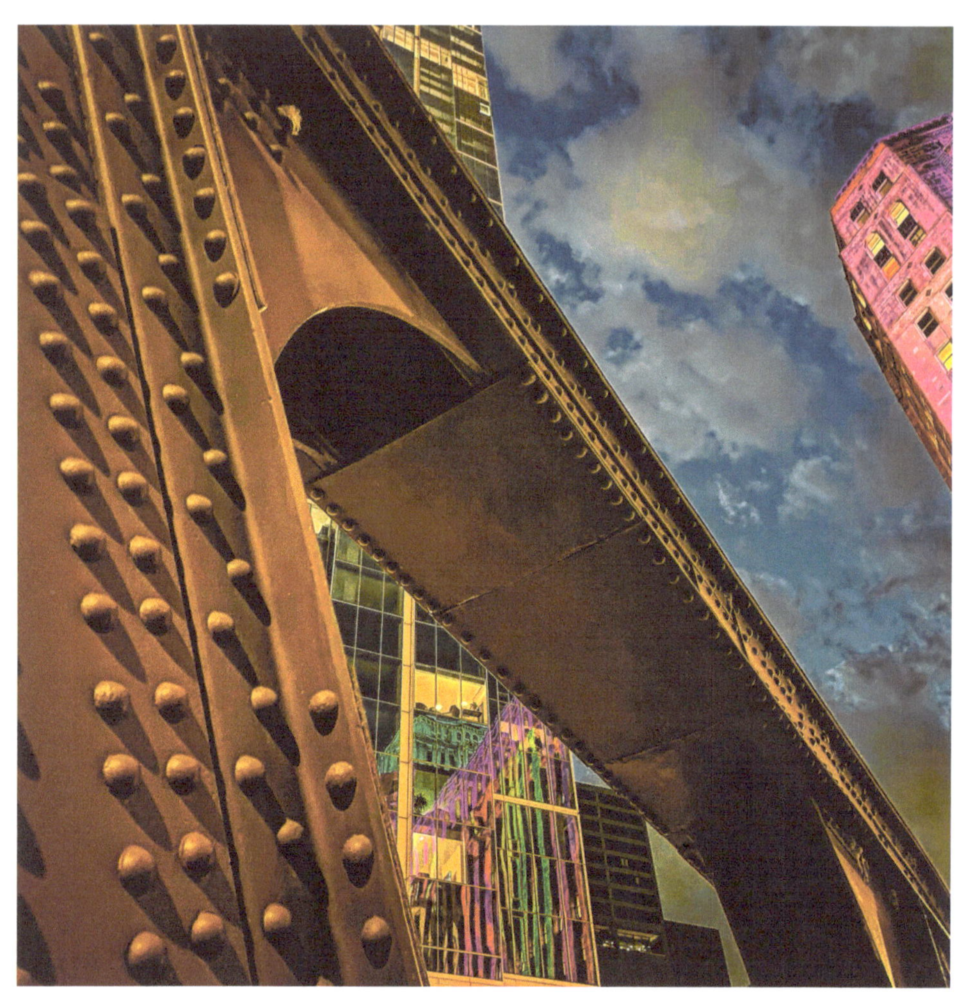

Inventions

We live where light and rust
Mount in measured layers
Like lovers without lust,
Or gods without prayers.
Who invented the bridge,
That fluvial sacrilege,
Or endless skyscrapers
Assailed by old newspapers?
They can't blot out the sky
Or dry up the rivers —
Just twist the eye awry
Till the brainstem quivers.
Throw light on slabs of glass
And vertigoes will pass.

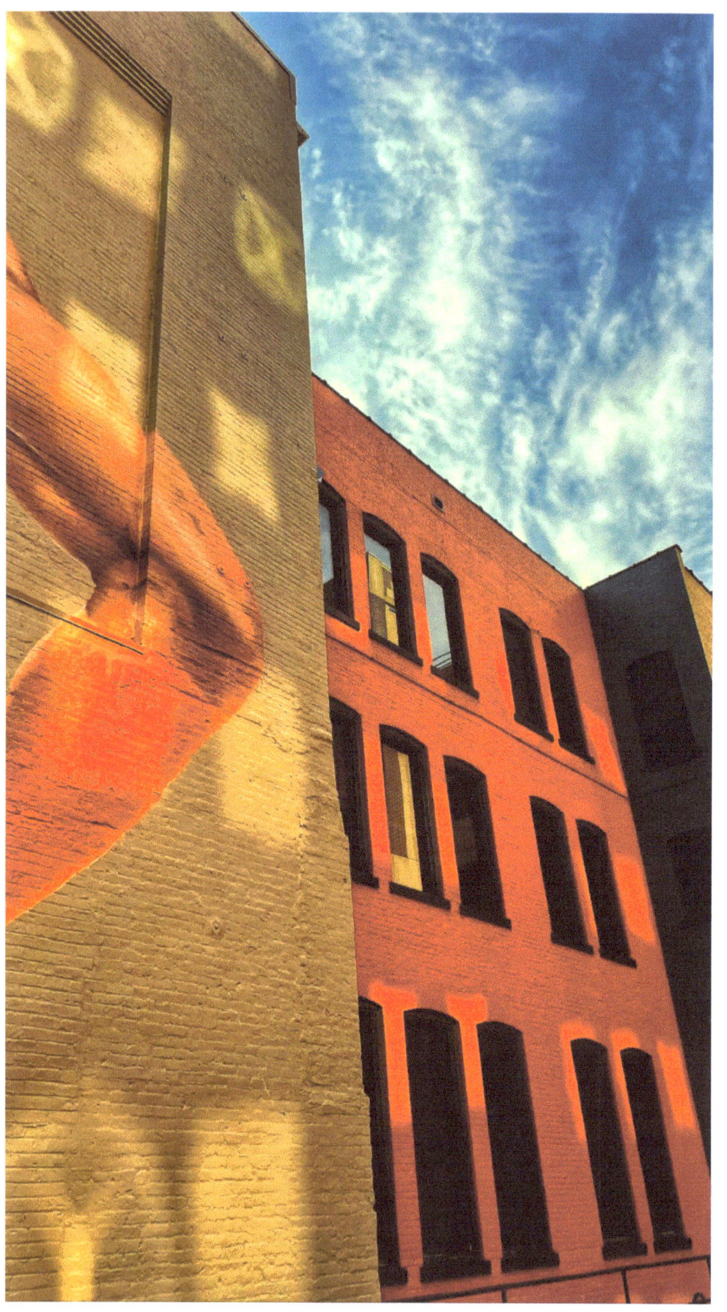

Grecian Elbow

Nature knows few right angles.
Man tends to abjure the curved.
Last night the moon swerved
To miss a cloud. The sun dangles.

The old white oak blown down,
Scattered its broken branches.
The wind passed on without a sound
In invisible avalanches.

Some windows are an open cage
Door with nothing inside to show.
Some walls mimic an empty page—
One's painted with a golden elbow.

We know nothing we don't realize
With or without our golden eyes.

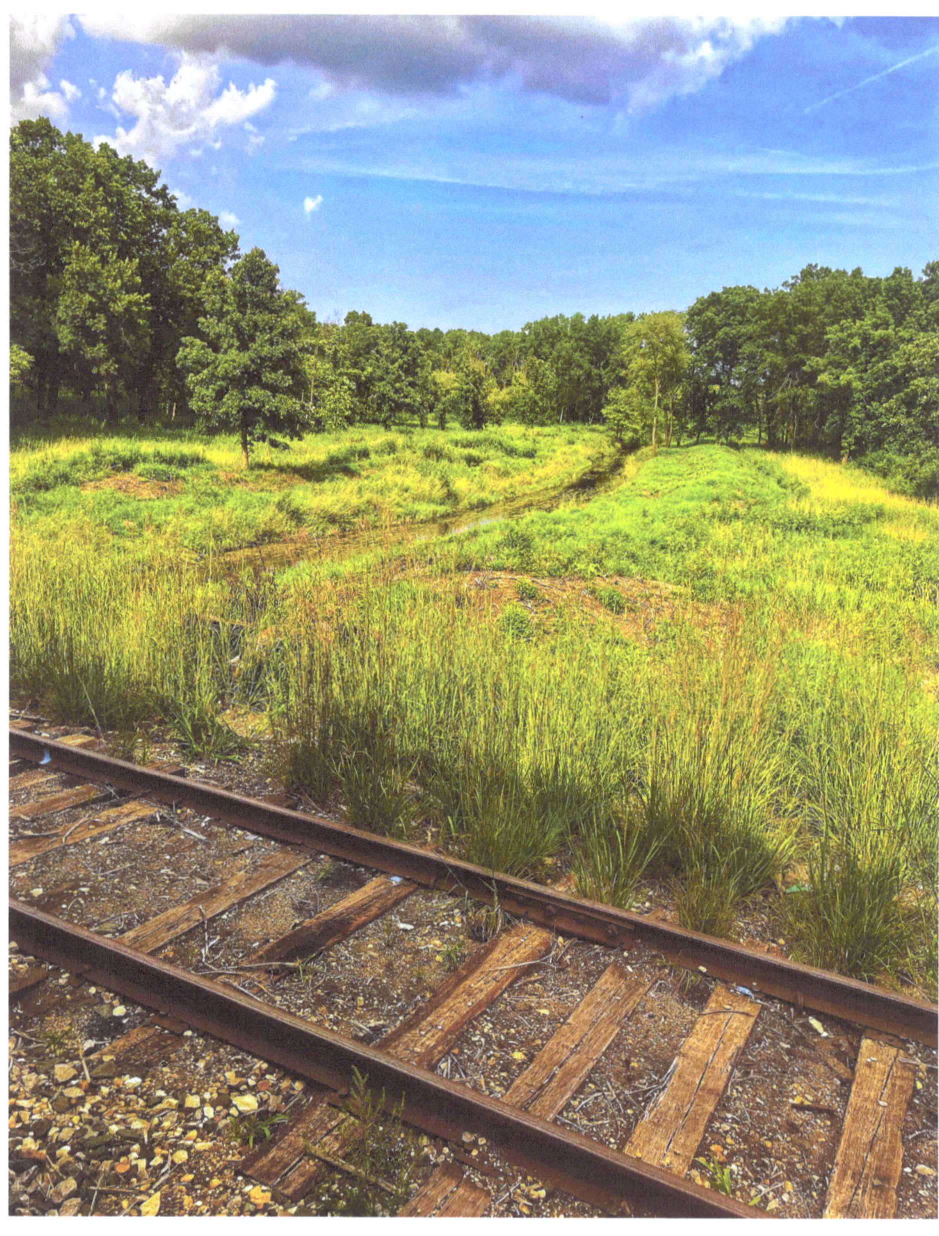

Path

The path into these woods begins
With tentative steps on bent grass
Widening for two to walk abreast.
The locomotives' blaring tocsins
Grow infrequent as the years pass.
Few paths reach a place unaddressed,
Though many have been abandoned.
(Van Gogh's led into wheat fields
Where all men's souls are pardoned
With the harvest's generous yields.)
It's hard to walk on railroad ties,
The first too close, the second too far.
I walk into woods, perhaps in error,
On a path that offers no alibis.

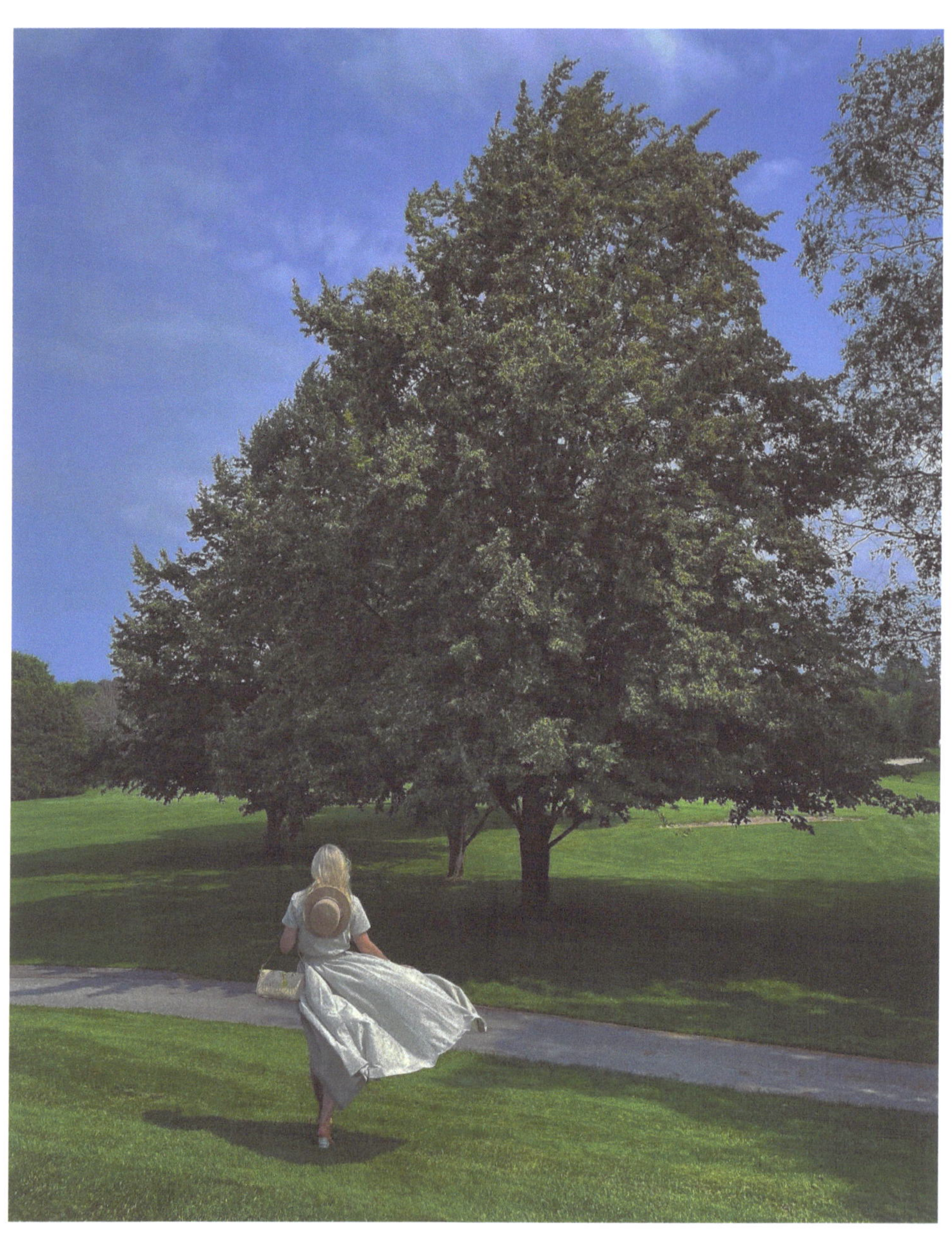

Woman and Wind

Eve listened to her heart and sinned,
Then passed out of paradise
Into paradise, clothed in wind,
Her mind unclouded as her eyes.
She found her husband hiding
Behind trees—he found her blinding.
They found each other in their arms
And recited a litany of charms.
They knew this world was not broken
And stood awaiting the awoken
Moment of their forgiveness.
Distant laughter beckoned them on.
As they walked beneath the midday sun,
The wind billowed her white silk dress.

The Essays

The Thing Itself is the Explanation

—Michael Antman

I wish to describe something impossible to describe.

When I was in my teens and early twenties, I sometimes would encounter an ordinary scene—for example, sunlight on an exposed brick wall—and I would be flooded with an instantaneous and involuntary physical sensation of pleasure, as if the sunlight had suddenly come to light inside of me.

This benevolently intense feeling was somewhat similar to the "chills" one gets upon reading a great poem or seeing an emotional scene in a movie, but I would feel it systemically, in every part of my body, and not just on the surface of my skin.

It was a sensation of inexplicable bliss, and it usually lasted a minute or two. Inexplicable, because the things I encountered were mundane and not commonly thought of as beautiful—brick walls, water towers, bare branches at mid-day or at dusk.

I wasn't thinking, in the way that amateur philosophers sometimes will condescend to all of creation, that "even a dead tree can be beautiful." In fact, I wasn't thinking at all. Nor was it a "spiritual" feeling, as if I were "at one with the world," or as if the world had suddenly revealed its essence to me. Both of these feelings would have required at least a degree of ratiocination, which was entirely absent in those moments.

Paradoxically, even though I experienced these unexpected encounters as a physical sensation, I felt at the same time as if my body weren't there, as if I had melted into the scene and the scene had melted into me. The experience would last anywhere from a few seconds to a few minutes, and then I'd go back to doing whatever I was doing.

There are other, very distantly kindred experiences such as "satori," or "epiphany," or "oceanic feeling" that entail a similar sensation of being separated from or transported out of one's quotidian self, but these other terms imply some form of realization —moments of intellectual or celestial revelation. In my compact raptures, nothing was revealed to me except, albeit very powerfully, the thing itself.

It was as if I were recalling the scene before me at the same instant that I was encountering it, happily (but only corporeally) recollecting something I thought had been lost—but where? when?—in vivid and intense detail. That elusive memory seemed to have great resonance and meaning for me, but was maddeningly beyond my ability to explain it, because I "understood" it only with my eyes and my body, and not with my mind.

The closest analogy I can think of is what the French call "jamais vu," the sudden sensation that you are encountering for the first time something you've seen many times before—though that wasn't quite it, either. Perhaps I was experiencing the world at these moments the way a baby does, the way it feels a deep delight at the vivid color of a building block. (I can still remember,

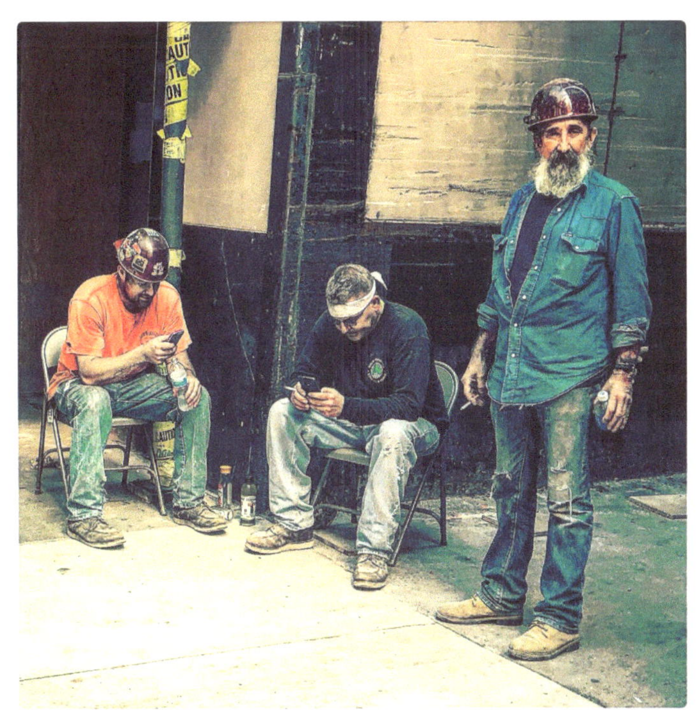

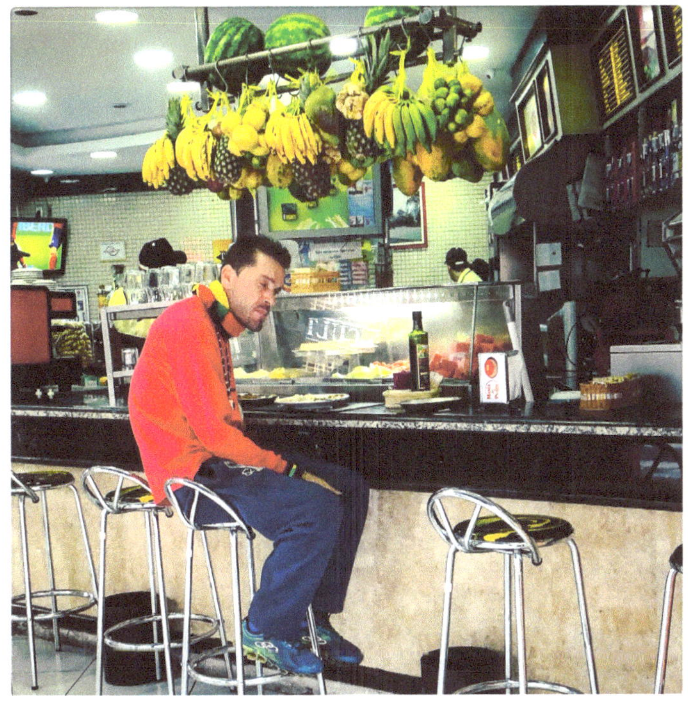

Previous page: Spontaneous photographs
Workmen (top) and *Sword of Bananocles* (bottom).

albeit very distantly, the intense pleasure I would get as a baby from staring at a bright red toy truck.)

This sensation was in large part what led me to write poetry—to not only describe this feeling in my poems but to attempt, with a great deal of youthful optimism, to evoke it in those who read the poems.

William Wordsworth was, I believe, attempting to express this very same feeling when he wrote:

"There was a time when meadow, grove, and stream,
  The earth, and every common sight,
To me did seem
Appareled in celestial light,
  The glory and the freshness of a dream..."

(The translator and poet Robert Fitzgerald describes this phenomenon, in his memoir of the same title, as "The Third Kind of Knowledge." He writes, looking back at his much younger self, that it was "a state of mind that very rarely befell me, but, when it did, seemed at once a superior kind of knowledge and an unearthly visitation...The state I refer to is not the same as a dream... it is quite definitely an extreme state of being awake.")

I wrote many poems—and passages in fiction and essays—that were attempts, at once, to recapture this evanescent sensation for myself, and to awaken it in others, just as Wordsworth had done so well in his poems. The limited degree to which I succeeded is secondary, however, to the even more limited degree to which, I now suspect, such sensations are even what the majority of readers are looking for when they seek out poetry or fiction.

I found the most success, I think, when I attempted to travel back to the root—to evoke the original feeling I had as a baby, when I apprehended the world with "the freshness of a dream" in a sort of pre-verbal fugue state:

Beginning with a Line by Me

From a map of breezes and pavement cracks
I built a shifting ghost-town in my brain.
It was never the same, that town, because
It was built of the breezes that crept across
Every web and weed I had ever dreamed.

It was a dog's dream, at that, for all I knew
Were the bucket, the stoop and the crippled bug
And the trembling threads in the nap of the rug.
Slight it was, and sweet, the bee-motioned breeze—
Ocean-scented, with the liquor of trees—

That led me around my deserted town,
Until speech detained me, and pulled me down,
And only a trace, evanescent, remained:
These fragrant streets, viewed from underneath,
Were a forgotten dream's white and twisted sheets.

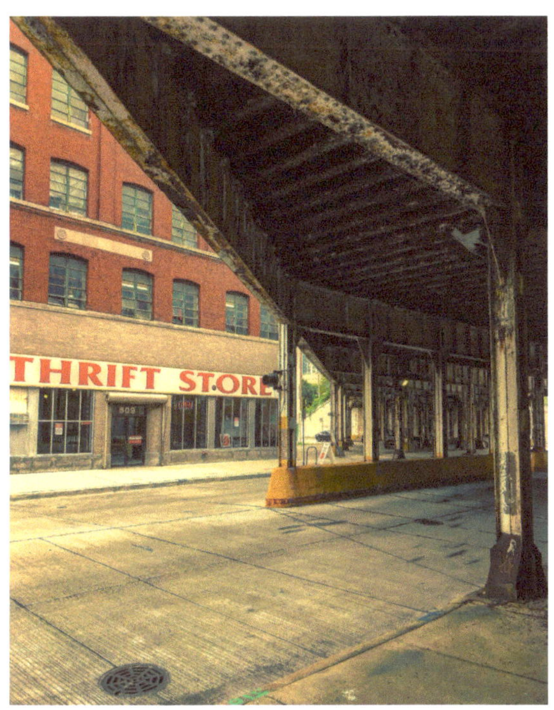
THRIFT STORE

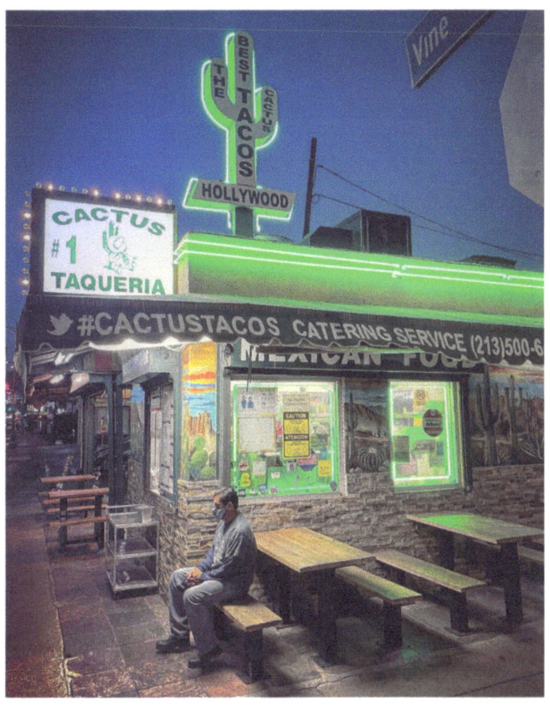
Vine
THE BEST TACOS
CACTUS
HOLLYWOOD
CACTUS
#1
TAQUERIA
#CACTUSTACOS CATERING SERVICE (213)500-6
MEXICAN FOOD

Previous page: Planned photographs *Recession* (top) and *Taco Stand* (bottom).

The phenomenon disappeared, as I recall, right around the time I took my first business trip, probably because I now had to pay more attention to things that were practical and useful—airline schedules and expense reports and the like—and less to things that were not. The sensation, to my regret, has never returned, and now, as I write about it for the first time, I can barely remember what it felt like, only that I *did* once feel it.

It is perhaps coincidental, and perhaps not, that I ceased writing poetry not long after this, too. Poetry, some have claimed, is a young person's game. More likely, I think, is that whatever freshness of perception or preternatural sensitivity I possessed when those inexplicable fits of rapture would overtake me gradually eroded in the face of the daily demands, not without their own satisfactions, of earning a living and raising a family.

In other words—to pick up where Wordsworth left off:

"…It is not now as it hath been of yore;—
 Turn wheresoe'er I may,
 By night or day.
The things which I have seen I now can see no more."

I continued to write fiction, but the primary purpose became, for me, not to evoke a feeling in the reader that rhymed with the way I (once) experienced the physical world, but rather to create characters who, by their conflicting goals and inborn contradictions, created a sort of internal combustion that drove a compelling narrative.

As I look back, the question that nags at me is why, at the time, I took the long way around, which is to say, why I attempted to turn this ineffable sensation into poetry—rather than to simply photograph the sites that elicited that sensation to begin with.

One reason was, as I look back on it, disappointingly mundane. Back then, camera equipment was heavy and bulky, and the thought of fumbling with a camera and lenses while adjusting the settings to capture a sight that was fleeting, unpredictable, and only partly visual in nature—it was as much inside of me as it was a part of the external world—strikes me as faintly absurd. I am glad that I didn't waste those moments of unexpected pleasure trying to capture them; it would have been like trying to photograph a dream.

In any event, the photographs I began taking not too many years ago—beginning in about 2014—were not really another attempt to recapture that long-gone feeling, nor to recreate it in the mind of the viewer (though if any of my photographs did end up doing that, it would be gratifying.) I was motivated, instead, by a feeling that would be best described as only adjacent to, and a pale simulacra of, my earlier perceptions—merely a pleasant appreciation for the overlooked, the ungainly, and the quotidian, the abandoned stretch of track briefly spotlit by the sun.

It is no coincidence that I took up photography at the same time that smartphone cameras became widely available. For, unlike traditional cameras, cellphone cameras allow you to take photos anywhere you go, and at a moment's notice. As such, they allow

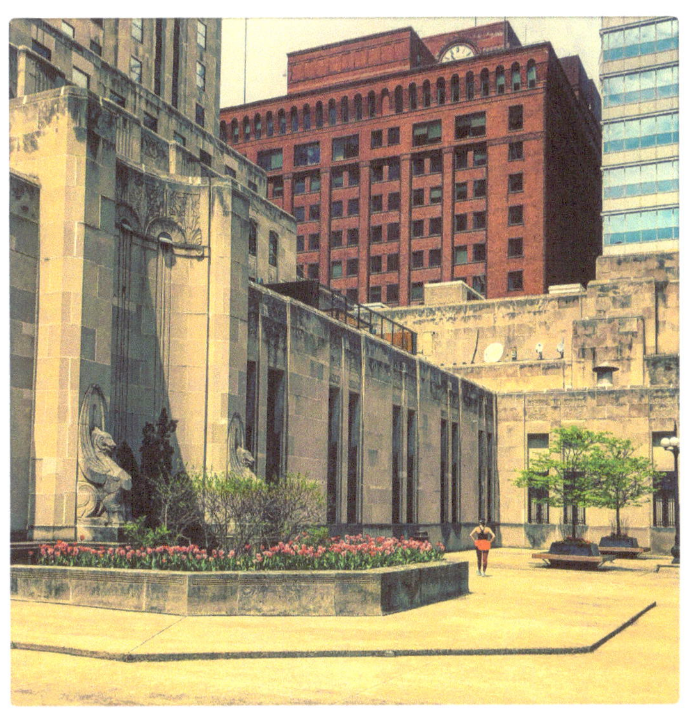

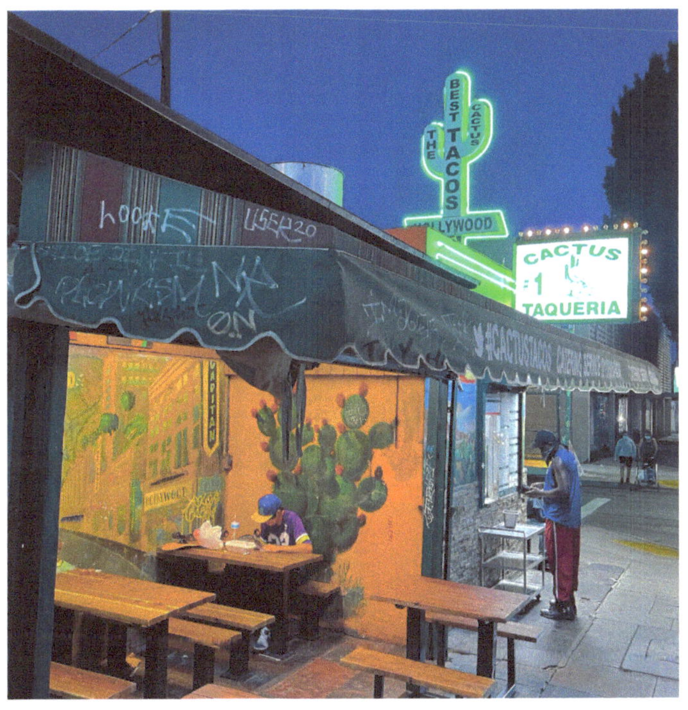
THE BEST CACTUS TACOS
CACTUS
TAQUERIA
#CACTUSTACOS

Previous page: Semi-spontaneous photographs *Woman in Tutu* (top) and *Study Session* (bottom).

for instantaneity—and it was that quality of unanticipated fleetingness that most haunted me about my youthful experiences. I look at my photographs now, and while they don't—and can't—recreate that earlier sensation of inexplicable bliss, they do, at least, sometimes capture the unexpectedness and the serendipity of it.

Many of these photos bring me pleasure in recollection precisely because if I had arrived a second earlier or a second later—if I had attempted to will them into existence—I would certainly have failed. Others of these photos are more "studied"—I came across a scene, and took my time with framing it. (See the photos accompanying this essay for examples of planned, spontaneous and semi-spontaneous photos I've taken.)

Either way, each photo—I've posted more than 4,200 to date to Instagram—is not only a satisfying act of capture or creation, but also a victory against memory and its inevitable losses, recompense for my inability to recapture a long-ago feeling that I no longer know how to feel.

Put in more general terms, I believe that most art, in essence, is a frustrated attempt to explain the inexplicable (a category that comprises both the transcendental and the seemingly banal, two phenomena that overlap to a considerable degree.)

But it is the attempt that moves us.

I believe that Christopher Guerin, in his poetry, is also attempting to explain, and evoke, some things that are inexplicable. After all, if it were easily explained, why would we need an explanation?

The poetry is the explanation. And, in his use of photography and other images as a springboard for his reflections, he in each case has created something more than the sum of its parts—a new kind of art that creates powerful synergies of sense and sensibility. The poems don't "explain" the photographs. And the photographs certainly don't explain the poems. In each case they combine to create something entirely different, something that cannot be reconstituted or rehydrated into prosaic explications.

The poetry alone, the photographs alone and, especially, the two together, are, in this book, saying the same thing to any who choose to engage with it, something that could very well serve as this book's epigraph—or its envoi:

"*I wished to describe something impossible to describe.*"

On Ekphrastic Poetry, "Inspiration," & the Sonnet

—Christopher Guerin

The eleven poems and photographs in this volume are part of a much larger work on the writer's part: more than 600 sonnets, all of which are paired with images—reproductions of paintings, photographs, drawings, prints, and sculpture. *My Human Disguise* is the title for this work of more than 12 years' effort. (It is available in its entirely on my blog, *Zealotry of Guerin.)*

"Collaboration" is the apt term for this book, since Michael Antman, an avid photographer, and I have been friends since 1972, and we worked jointly to create each pairing of poem and image. In 2015, I was struck by his photo *Crossing*, which then became Sonnet #250 of *My Human Disguise*. Over the next eight years ten more sonnets followed, responding in differing ways to Michael's photographs.

As the reader will discover, there is no theme running through the photographs, nor the sonnets. My selection of Michael's eleven photos, which he published on Instagram and, less often, on Facebook, was as much a matter of serendipity as anything. Each photo simply stood out as being interesting in a way that made me to want to fashion a sonnet to stand next to it. The collaboration was in the selection of a title, which was usually a joint effort, and Michael's application of his fine-tuned ear to my poems, bringing about an occasional change in the language. The idea of publishing this volume was Michael's.

The purpose of this essay is in part to debunk the idea that poems are "inspired." In fact, the more I've written sonnets for *My Human Disguise*, the more I've come to find suspect the words "inspired" and "ekphrasis." (Ekphrasis refers to the use of detailed description of an image for poetic effect.)

How many authors have been confronted with the tired question: "What inspires you to write?" and, more specifically, "What inspired you to write that (poem, novel, short story, etc.)?" I object to the word today because it is both imprecise, and misleading.

It's as if readers suspect some mysterious or even mystic force (or being) whispers in the author's ear, or in his dreams, or taps his brain and inserts some idea or image. What actually happens, quite simply, is that in observing the world, and thinking about what is observed, combined with the author's own opinions and determinations of what the world is and what it isn't, what is interesting, what is right or wrong, good or bad, clear or murky, etc., he or she begins to put words to paper. Yes, one can be prompted by an image, or a natural phenomenon, or someone else's own thoughts and ideas, to begin to write, but "prompted" is about as close as I'm willing to get to "inspired" when I think about why I write what I do. (I'm close to disingenuousness here, because I am presenting poems, sonnets specifically, always in tandem with an image.)

So what is my relationship to the images in this volume and throughout *My Human Disguise*?

There are probably as many answers as images in *My Human Disguise*, but I can group them into a more manageable number.

The image sometimes comes first and the poem later. But I often have an idea for a poem and go looking for an image to pair it with.

Once I have selected an image, the poem can take any one of several approaches. Probably least often do I act according to the definition of "ekphrasis." I seldom "use" detailed description of the content of the image to construct the sonnet. I might use words that the image suggests, but I don't describe the image in detail, to create a sort of verbal mirror of the image. I'm more likely to create a narrative or commentary that somehow, often loosely, relates to the image.

W.H. Auden's "Musee des Beaux Arts," which is based on Breughel's *The Fall of Icarus*, is probably the most famous of ekphrastic poems, and it does use extensive detailed description of the painting's contents for poetic effect. This is something I don't often do.

Rather, I use the image as a stepping off point for my own purposes, or for applying my own interpretation of the image. I might comment on the image, or allude to some aspect of the image, but more often the sonnet takes a direction that has virtually nothing to do (or has only a tangential relationship) with the image.

Here is my version of *The Fall of Icarus*, which appears as Sonnet #302, based on a painting by Picasso, but virtually ignores Picasso's treatment of the subject.

The sun is father to the father and the son.
Maze-minded Daedalus almost invented Earth;
If it was (and it had to be) born, his reason
Rolled it into a ball of life and roaring mirth.
He knew what was needed, met the exigencies
Of power over nature and control of fate,
The harnessing of the mind and how it foresees,
The imprisoning of evil, the murder of hate.
He must have been a loving father, or a fool,
To fashion wings for his son as well as himself.
We know, he warned the boy, that they were just a tool
To scratch the sky, not calipers to span the gulf
Between dirt and light. The heedless boy died too soon,
To his earth-glad father a stripped and distant moon.

Why, then, you might ask, pair your sonnets with images at all, if the relationship between them is only tangential?

Artistically, quite aside from content, my intention, my belief, is that poem and image combined provide a more immersive experience than either poem or image would on its own.

I'm speaking in the context of a printed book. Obviously, images are intended to stand on their own. Picasso, Cezanne or

Klee didn't anticipate, and might actually dislike, the idea of their works being published side by side with a sonnet. (The purposeful illustration of books, of course, by Picasso and many other artists, is a different matter altogether.)

My presumption, though, is confined, as it is in this volume, to the poem and the image being presented simultaneously, available for cross-referral or comparison, or simple, mutual illustration (to the extent that words can illustrate an image).

The relationship is not always equal (though that isn't the case in this volume) and the image, even a famous one, can take a subordinate role. Yet this is merely a matter of emphasis, and what the reader chooses to take from the pairing. My hope, though, is to provide a novel, and sometimes even startling, experience of the purposeful mingling of image and words.

The Sonnet

The poet Rita Dove has written that formal poetry—such as the sonnet—is "a bejeweled casket"—a phrase I admire for its cleverness, though I hardly agree with, given the contents of this book. It's like saying the realistic novel, or the one-act play, or the long short story are all dead as art forms. The sonnet is just one of many, equally valid, ways in which to write poetry.

Though there are many sonnet forms—some claiming the form for no other reason than being 14 lines long—mine don't follow any one rhyme or metrical scheme. Rather, I follow a few basic rules.

Any kind of rhyme scheme is acceptable as long as no rhyme is more than 3 lines apart (a rule I break only once). In most cases, a rhyme ceases to be a rhyme if the two rhyming words are too far apart to resonate.

A sonnet can have any mix of rhyme patterns. A single sonnet's scheme can be, for example, ABC ABC DD EE FGGF (or FGFG), or any variation of those. Some sonnets can be all couplets, some three quatrains and a couplet, or even use the same rhyme for all fourteen lines.

I work in four meters, composed of "feet" of two beats: trimeter, tetrameter, pentameter, or hexameter. In my later sonnets, many lines have an additional beat, though I'm always hoping to have the line land on a pleasing end rhythm. I am not fussy about where the accents fall. Most feet are iambic, with the accent on the second syllable, but I often vary accents for my own reasons, having to do with the meaning or music of the poem.

Stanzas are primarily couplets, tercets, quatrains, or sestets, and I often ignore the much vaunted "volta" (when, after the sixth or eigth line, the poem takes a sudden turn.)

I never distort or reverse normal syntax in order to rhyme. For centuries it was okay to back into a rhyme in formal poetry. In other words, it was considered a proper tool of poetry to write in a manner different from the way in which we talk to each other.

For example, I would never distort syntax as Shelley does in the second and third lines from his "Ode to the West Wind":

O wild West Wind, thou breath of Autumn's being,
Thou, from whose unseen presence the leaves dead
Are driven, like ghosts from an enchanter fleeing...

I have been writing formal, rhyming poetry for decades, though not exclusively. Rhymes, I believe, are not only pleasing to the ear, they are a means of both connecting and generating ideas. Perhaps others predetermine the words they plan to rhyme before even beginning, but I doubt it. Words beget rhymes and rhymes beget more rhymes.

And it's no game. Some words have virtually no rhyming partner words; others have dozens. A serious poet avoids the obvious and cliched rhyme (moon, june, tune, soon, etc.), making writing sonnets (or any other form of rhyming poetry) a great, but extremely rewarding challenge. At times, an obvious rhyme is the appropriate rhyme, but the writer must be careful to make clear its special necessity in a context that is not a cliché.

Others have written that writing poetry is a process of discovery —I think never more so than when the author teases out rhyme after rhyme in order to compose a complete work.

I'll conclude with a sonnet dedicated to Michael, #200, based on my own photograph (of stones collected in New Zealand by my daughter Alice), from September 2014, in appreciation of his editing *My Human Disguise,* which goes all the way back to the first sonnet in 2011. It's perhaps the best expression of what *My Human Disguise* is all about.

Question

1

My daughter brought these stones from New Zealand.
At first we arranged them in a circle,
The white veins touching, mostly, band to band.
They seemed to me a kind of miracle,
Holding everything we know inside,
And all we don't brought in from far and wide.
But soon that seemed too pat an arrangement,
With a history, yes, and silent, but,
However Zen-like, it didn't hit my gut.
The circle must be cut open and bent,
As the thing it did not contain, allow,
Was questions (the world just is, here and now?).
The stones, like this 200th sonnet, speak,
And answer with a question what we seek.

2

To ask or not to ask, that is to be.
No answer has been satisfactory.
I can't know the secrets of my own soul,
Because, like Richard Wilbur's star-nosed mole,

I can only pass by the graves of men,
Whose own souls, if at last revealed to them,
May be whispering, like wind in the grass—
Language meant only for the dead *en masse*.
Instead, I'll ask for nothing but the sun
To answer with its rising tomorrow,
And listen to cicadas, one by one,
Respond with obliterated sorrow.
I love you all. That's an answer for now.
Someday I might learn more. I'll let you know.

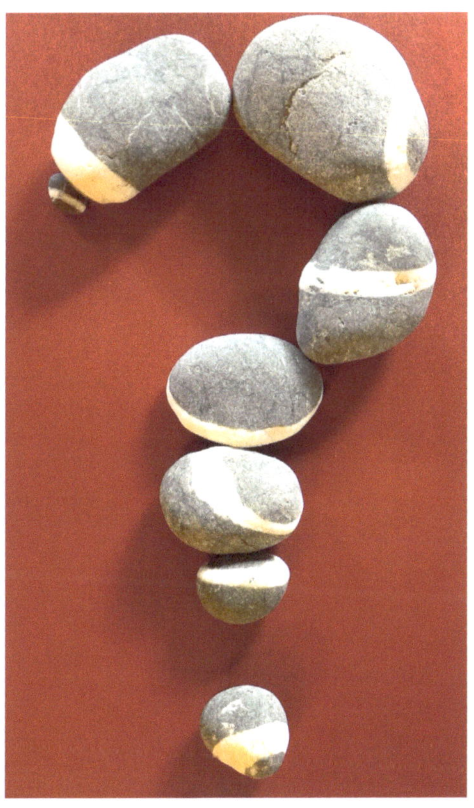

Michael Antman is a former senior marketing executive, an urban photographer, a theatre and book critic, and the author of the novels *Everything Solid Has a Shadow* and *Cherry Whip*, and the memoir *Searching for the Seagull Motel.* He also is an English-language editor of a Russian dissident literary magazine by and for opponents of the Putin regime. His essay on Vladimir Nabokov's last novel, *The Original of Laura*, can be found in the critical anthology *Shades of Laura* by the Nabokov scholar Yuri Leving. He is a two-time finalist for the National Book Critics Circle Nona Balakian Award for Excellence in Reviewing. His photography can be found on Instagram @michaelantman, and his author's website is michaelantman.com.

Christopher Guerin has two degrees in English Literature from Northern Illinois University. He spent 26 years in the symphony orchestra business, 20 as the President of the Fort Wayne Philharmonic. His stories and poems have appeared in the following literary magazines: *RE:AL, Wind, Windless Orchard, AURA, Wittenberg Review, riverrun, Midwest Quarterly, Roanoke Review, New Collage, SEEMS, DEROS, Rosebud, Towers, Rectangle, Re:Markings, Flying Island, Hopewell Review, The William and Mary Review, sou'wester*, and *Oxford Magazine* (Miami University, Oxford, Ohio). His poems "The House" and "Orion" were published in *A World Assembly of Poets* (Nibir Ghosh, Phd. ed), with the likes of Paul Muldoon, Rita Dove, and Ariel Dorfman. His book of his first 200 ekphrastic sonnets, *My Human Disguise*, was published by Voca Me Press in 2016. To date, *My Human Disguise* includes more than 600 sonnets. He is the author of two volumes of short stories published by Amika Press, *The Story of My Universe* and *Loverless Love*. His one-act plays, *Quartet* and *Cat Murder*, will be staged in the spring of 2024.

www.ingramcontent.com/pod-product-compliance
Lightning Source LLC
LaVergne TN
LVHW052256100826
845147LV00001B/57

* 9 7 9 8 2 1 8 2 7 9 7 4 5 *